Living Free Within Myself

Living Free Within Myself

Darrell Summerville

"Love has no bounds, for it is fueled by faith."

- *Kendrick Jones*

LIVING FREE
WITHIN MYSELF
By Darrell Summerville

Authorship Publishing, LLC
ATTENTION: Permissions Department,
Suite 120 - 128
Irving, TX 75063

Printed in the United States of America
BY
Authorship Publishing, LLC
Dallas, TX

This book is dedicated to my wife and family,
who have supported me throughout this vision.
I am what I am because of your undying love and support.

Dear Reader,

I'd first like to say welcome....Welcome to the first day of the rest of your life!! You have taken the first step to experiencing the blessing of God's will for your life – and that is what we call FREEDOM...There is a quiet movement taking place and it speaks to us all individually, yet with the same message and subtle intensity. What you are about to experience is what I like to call, "A church without walls", so sit back and prepare yourself to take it all in.

They say that "words travel fast", I never understood that concept until after writing this book. I now know what is meant by "the Word travels fast". Many people have said to me, that while reading this book it felt as though I am sitting there with them. I'm here to tell you that there IS someone sitting there, but it is not me. What you will experience is the presence of the One that calmed my hands to write this message. A message that I pray, will release you from depression, fear, anger or any other feeling of inadequacy.

Thank you for taking the time out to read, **"Living Free Within Myself"**. I ask that, if you find this book brings forth healing or helps you in any way, place it in the hands of someone you care about. Someone who may need to believe that, they too can make it beyond any struggle they are currently facing. This is a message of freedom, so pass it along my friend.

With Love,

Darrell Summerville

Contents

Introduction

Being free actually starts in conception. Each individual is born free, but it is only when responsibility is understood and accepted that we become shackled. Before you had the responsibility of paying for something or being somewhere, it was a wonderful feeling to live without a care in the world. That moment of innocence is a wonderful time to understand yourself; at this point, life becomes an oyster of information. Parents, it is exactly for this reason that we should teach our children to learn more of who they are while they have the chance before life impresses upon them a label that it wants them to have which most times does not fit. When life's obstacles are thrown in your path, it may be too late to discover your purpose or your reason for being. When you are late finding yourself, while having to endure responsibility, is when the struggle truly begins. This is where we usually dig deeper holes because we are trying to catch up.

When you were a child, what did you want to be when you grew up? Have you reached your dream? If a child tells you what they want to be when they grow up, it is pure and without confinements. Understanding parents find out what it is their children want to be and set them on a path to achieve their dream. Very few kids tell you they simply want to be rich, but they tell you the type of occupation they would like to have. However, somewhere during the process of growing up, we have allowed people to place upon us what they would like us to be, and now we have to live our lives while trying to figure out someone else's dream.

If we have not learned to be free, then life is unknown territory. It is as if from one day to another, we do not know who we will be the next day, the next hour, or the next second. Life changes and we have to move with the changes. Without knowing yourself, how can you position yourself? Positioning yourself to be where you are destined to be is critical, just as recognizing when your time is at hand is critical. As a matter of fact, it is the first step to finding your purpose. When you are on time for God's purpose for you, then you are able to function in a higher element. And when you are able to function in this element, you have a more natural ability for your belief and hope to become faith.

What is your time? Your time is when you understand where you are, who you are, and more importantly where you fit in this moment of your life. A mind that has not been freed cannot free another. If I have gotten lost along the way then the only directions that I can give to you are the directions that I have taken, which have gotten me lost as well. We ask our friends (who are usually in a worst predicament than we are) to help, but we are asking them the impossible. This is when we begin choosing our friends that are able to encourage us or tell us what we want to hear, rather than those who are honest with us. It is a true statement, "The truth will set you free".

In discovering yourself and gaining your freedom no one said the road would be easy. If it were easy, then we all would be free and there would be no need for any self-help books. Freedom starts with a self-evaluation of one's own self and ends with an acceptance of change. With this understanding, you can begin to live free within yourself.

Reflection

1. Think back to when you were a child. What did you want to become when you grew up? Who did you most see yourself as?

2. Is this image a reflection of who you are today? If not, what is it that keeps you from seeing yourself as that person?

3. At this point in your life, are you willing to move forward towards your freedom?

Breaking New Ground

Breaking new ground is not an easy task, especially if you are accustomed to doing things a certain way your whole life. Habits (especially bad) harden fertile soil. To become free one must be ready, as change is inevitable in the freedom process. Change allows growth, and growth allows you to keep up with the changes in life no matter how rigid they are. Change is usually seen as negative because as human beings, we do not like the uncomfortable feelings that change tends to bring. However, God assures us that He will be with us in our hardships.

> *"Let your conduct be without covetousness; be content with such things as you have." For He Himself has said, 'I will never leave you nor forsake you.' So we may boldly say: 'The Lord is my helper; I will not fear. What can man do to me?" (Hebrews 13: 5 & 6 – NKJV)*

This is a promise that God has made to us, and while we are breaking that dry hard soil, we can know that God is there helping us break through. However, you must believe that promise in order for it to work for you.

For example, in the parable of the farmer and the seed, God has given us a plan for success. In order for the farmer to be successful in his environment, he had to know the ground, the season for the ground to be tilled, and the season for the seed to be planted. But more importantly, he had to know how to wait on the harvest. It is important to wait on the harvest because we try to rush God. When we are impatient, we move past the harvest and wonder why someone else has come behind us gathering the fruits of our labor.

I keep mentioning "hard soil" and unless you are a farmer you may not understand this concept initially or how this applies to you; therefore, let me explain. Hard soil is the equivalent of being stubborn or what most of us call being "hard-headed". It is your ideas and your heart that God must come into and make fertile. This is not to be seen as a negative or to make you feel guilty. Life's struggles and burdens cause the soil to harden, but new thoughts and new direction have the power to loosen that hardness. Breaking new ground means you are saying that you are getting ready to go somewhere different in your life, but in order to do that you must be ready to understand something new in your life.

The ground is our outward perception of life and it is directly connected to our five senses. What we smell, touch, taste, hear, and see directly impacts the condition of our soil. Negative life experiences tend to cause hardening of the ground. When we use our natural intelligence to understand God's plan for us it causes us to belittle ourselves. What I mean by this is, what God has for us is great and when He reveals a small portion of it to us, we are in awe because we are trying to perceive this with our natural mind. We simply don't know how His plan for us could possibly happen. It is then that we start to doubt and it is this very doubt that causes depression to sink its filthy claws into our souls.

The seed is what God has placed in us. God's seed can be a direction, a goal, or an objective, but the perfect word to define it is "Purpose". Purpose tells us "What I am in this life." For purpose to be placed into action there must be a change. However, initially when we think of change, by default we think of pain because we see ourselves having to be moved out of our comfort zones. By human nature, we all want to be comfortable; no one goes out of their way to make themselves uncomfortable.

Change is simply shifting from one level to a higher level. Change in a person's life should be seen as positive opposed to negative. When we are breaking new ground, it is not intended for us to lessen ourselves, it is for us to better ourselves. God is all about change. There are too many levels in God for us to remain at one. Breaking new ground is a necessity to move forward in God.

God is the farmer that prepares the ground for the seed to take. He softens the ground by breaking it up in order to plant His seed within you. In other words, God puts us in situations that make us uncomfortable so the seed, which is His message, can be planted within us. His seed must be planted deep within so that the "crows" (instruments of Satan) do not come in and rob us of God's seed.

We should also realize that sometimes God **allows** havoc to come into our lives so that we have the ability to replant. In order to grow in God and have success in life, we have to allow God or the Holy Spirit to break things up in our lives. These things that require breaking could very well be the negative life experiences, the hurts, and the pain that have hardened us.

Now, if God is the farmer in the previous example, then the Holy Spirit is the shovel or tiller God uses. Yes, God comes into our lives to remove the things that hinder us. Some of the hindrances are past hurts, low self esteem, rejections, and life's struggles. We must understand that the bad hinders the good. A bad job keeps us away from a good job and a bad relationship keeps us away from a good relationship. God in His eternal wisdom uses the things that we see and feel as tragedies to take us to a higher level. Very few people experience change when they perceive things are going well. The very things that bind us and pull us away from God are the things that He comes in to remove so that we can be free from the bondage of life in order to allow our seeds to have a suitable environment for growth.

God has everything in control. He did not mean for life's "negative" experiences to harden us. His desire is for those experiences to expose us to new growth and allow us to understand the motivation of life. The bad relationship was not meant to make us give up on relationships as a whole; it was designed to help us recognize a bad relationship as well as the components that give life to a bad relationship. With this knowledge, you will be prepared when the person God sent to you comes into your life; the very person who would have otherwise been rejected because of hardened soil.

Understand that you cannot control your surroundings, but you have the ability to control yourself and how things affect you. This comes by discipline and sacrifice. Breaking new ground requires much discipline. One of the major problems of believers is the lack of discipline. It is when you achieve self-discipline everything else will be in its rightful place. For example, getting behind a steering wheel when you have had too much to drink cannot give the one who was drunk the confidence and peace to say that the accident was in God's will. However, when you have had nothing to drink and an accident happens - in other words, you have controlled what you could - can it then be said that the accident was meant to happen?

Discipline comes in several different ways, but in the end they are one and the same. Let me explain: Your relationship with God...*Do you have a relationship with Him? Do you know Him personally and intimately? Are you obedient to Him? Do you honor Him? Do you trust Him?* Being disciplined in your relationship with God automatically creates discipline within yourself.

Scripture refers to us first as natural and then spiritual. This means that you must first understand your functions as a human being before you can understand your functions as a spiritual being. In order for you to understand God, you must first understand what He created. You were created in His image and in His likeness, so once you understand yourself, then you have a better opportunity of understanding God. And when you have understood your own limitation, you can understand God's ability. When you know that you can't go on and you **must** trust God for strength, then you understand that the strength came from another source - God.

Discipline is a part of order, and since God is a God of order, then we as humans must be orderly for God does not work in disorder. Chaos is a man-made condition. In other words, God didn't bring the chaos we experience into our lives... we did. The Lord is bound by His word, and His word says He promised to help us in our time of need. It was never meant by God for mankind to grow out of our own understanding or in what we believe. We make the fatal mistake of trying to lean on our own understanding. Leaning

7

on our own understanding is like trying to carry an elephant on wet tissue. Scripture tells us:

> *"Trust in the Lord with all your heart, And lean not on your own understanding..." (Proverbs 3:5- NKJV)*

This is because when you shape your life out of your own understanding you tend to fall into a humanistic ideology. This becomes evident when you start to pull others away from God and draw them to yourself. In doing this, you make your struggles the struggles of others and your weaknesses the weaknesses of others. Also, when we are doing this, we give people a man-made plan that has inconsistencies and errors instead of God's perfect plan for us in which the details have already been worked out. Man-made plans leave out the details, but a perfect plan works out all the details. God's plan for us is a good and successful plan for our lives if we are willing to be disciplined and follow the perfect will of God for our lives. .

We have said that breaking new ground is not an easy task, but why isn't it easy for us? Only when a person is desperate will they find a reason to change. Breaking new ground is doing just that. It is going to the heart of the matter and saying, "I must change this hard surface." It was the same hardness we used to get through some situations in our lives, like a spouse cheating on us or some other loved one betraying us. Soil that was once soft, rich and fertile became hardened by "life". There is a danger of your soil being hardened for too long, because nothing penetrates hard soil and nothing comes out either. Look at your yard when it has not rained in years, the soil becomes so hard that it chokes the life out of any vegetation that attempts to grow. Yes, it kills the weeds that sprout up, but it also kills the grass and flowers as well. When it does rain the rain does not penetrate, it has to sit on the top of the soil for awhile. This water sitting on top of hard soil usually causes flash flooding in areas, and the water can rise high enough to flood and destroy our homes. This is the danger when nothing can penetrate you as well.

An example of danger is when a new friend that God has sent to you is cut off because some other friend that you picked hurt you. Or a spouse that God sent to you cannot penetrate your heart with their words and love because some person you picked before them cheated on you. This is especially true for women. Many people do not understand what women go through when they are hurt. For women, pain goes down to the core of their being. If you are built on emotions, then the very fabric of you is also hurt when someone scars you. There are women out there who are now trying to have babies but are unsuccessful. They go to their physician, spending thousands of dollars for artificial insemination, with no success. They never come to the understanding that the gift of life comes from God. They don't realize that hard soil chokes out life and the womb becomes barren because of it. If you have tried the same things over and over and haven't gotten any results, then try something new. Forgive those people in your past that have hurt you. Honor God and His words, for they bring forth life.

Don't give your forgiveness because you want to have the child, but do it because it glorifies the Lord and bring forth freedom in your life. You will find out that if you are not able to give, then you are not able to receive, for they are one in the same door. There is a child that is waiting on you, a husband that is waiting on you, or a friend that will stick closer to you than a brother or a sister waiting on you.

Make no mistake about it, once you forgive those that have hurt you, and once you let go of the hatred that has grown into you, you will feel naked. You will feel like you are weakened and that someone could hurt you... Ultimately, you will feel vulnerable. During this time it is important that you get more into your Bible and start studying the characteristics of God and what He says His people are to be. So that when someone comes to you that do not have the characteristics of God, you can let them pass on by. Where we are naked, God will clothe us in His armor.

> *"Finally, be strong in the Lord and in His mighty power. Put on the full armor of God so that you take your stand against the devil's schemes. For our*

struggle is not against flesh and blood, but against the rulers, against the authorities, against the power of this dark world and against the spiritual forces of evil in the heavenly realms. Therefore, put on the full armor of God so that when the day of evil comes, you may be able to stand your ground, and after you have done everything to stand. Stand firm then, with the belt of truth buckled around your waist, with the breastplate of righteousness in place, and with your feet fitted with the readiness that comes from the gospel of peace. In addition to all of this, take up the shield of faith, with which you can extinguish all the flaming arrows of the evil one. Take the helmet of salvation and sword of the Spirit, which is the word of God. And pray in the Spirit on all occasions with all kinds of prayers and requests. With this in mind, be alert and always keep on praying for all the saints." *(Ephesians 6:10 – 18- NKJV)*

My dear brothers and sisters, when you feel naked God will clothe you with His armor. The scripture above never said that the devil will stop or that you will not have to endure any of his the schemes, but it does tell us how to defend ourselves from the attacks.

Reflection

1. Identify the life experiences that have caused you to become "hardened".

2. What habits have you adopted that has helped you deal with those experiences as well as contributed to the "hardness" in your life?

3. Are you willing to trust God with the experiences that have hardened you?

4. Do you have a relationship with Him? Do you know Him personally and intimately?

Don't quite know how or what to do to form a relationship with God? Email me at: livingfree@authorshippublishing.com

Breaking New Ground

Reader's Notes

_____

_____

_____

_____

_____

_____

_____

_____

_____

_____

_____

_____

Keep It Moving

The main processes in realizing your potential and freeing yourself is the art of movement. Movement has always been tied to the physical and there are many writers who have already spoken about the physical movement of the body, but what I would like to discuss is the spiritual movement that must take place. Both practices of movement help us in our daily lives because they both bring forth positive energy. When I use the phrase "Keep It Moving", I am simply saying that "***I am more than a conqueror; I will not allow anything to hold me down!***"

If you are moving in the physical sense, then you are saying that you will not allow anything to attach itself to you. Everything physical can only hang on to you for a moment, for your physical movement seeks to detach physical things from you. Let us delve deeper so you understand where we are going.

The very enemy of any relationship, marriage, or achieving a dream is doing "nothing", or non-movement. Life is perpetual motion, constant movement. If you allow yourself to become stagnated, life can and will literally pass you by. With constant motion, comes constant surprises and unless you can understand life in this manner, life becomes nearly impossible to plan for or to even understand. As life moves, you move also.

God is pure movement and He operates in a timely motion. He may be ready to deliver your blessing to you at a predestined time and in a predestined place, but if you are not moving with God you will miss your blessing. For example, if you are stressed about a financial blessing, God is getting the check in the mail. God knows this and therefore, has set about orchestrating the steps to get it to you. Those steps involve someone putting the check in the mail, someone delivering the check to you, and you being there to accept the check. All of these things must be in place. Now, a good question to ask is "What happens if the check is being delivered, and I never come back home?" Well, you will simply miss the check (your blessing). In order to fulfill your purpose for this time in life, then **YOU** must be moving with God for He does not move with us.

There is a part of spiritual movement that if you are unprepared causes you to give up or give in. Movement brings about growth and in this spiritual growth period we are taken to a new level which takes us from the comfortable stage we were just in. In this stage, there is pain felt for the man and the woman of God. Even in your physical growth, we have identified that there are "growing pains". The pain associated with this growth is only for a short time while we are adjusting to the change. The spiritual growth periods are when God allows "bad things" to happen in our lives, not to kill us, but to bring us to a different level within Him that benefit our lives. These obstacles strengthen us because the spiritual man needs it to grow. To know that God is strengthening you through these challenges and that they are only for a period of time is meant to inspire you. This time is not to make you quit or become frustrated. You are only going through the circumstance in order to help you get to and to go through to the next level in your life.

Are you constantly going through the same obstacle in your life? You must move in the spirit for the growth to take place. In some cases, you have to move in the physical aspect that causes growth. For example, there are friends, acquaintances and/or family members that you must remove from your life in order to be blessed. These people may be carrying a weight of negativity and confusion that impacts your life so much that it causes setbacks in your life. If you're finding yourself being challenged with the same obstacles, move some people around to see if the challenge comes to an end.

> *"I press toward the goal for the prize of the upward call of God in Jesus Christ..." (Philippians 3:14 – NKJV)*

This scripture encourages us to press toward the mark for the prize of the high calling of God in Christ Jesus. This means that we are always pressing onward to the things that God has promised us through Christ Jesus. We must keep moving in our good days and bad days, especially when we do not feel like it. Because of the great calling God has on our lives and the prize that is waiting for us, just to know that the Almighty God is calling all of us to a higher level is motivating enough for me. I believe that whatever the reason that God keeps pushing us must be great if God is the one doing the pushing.

The visible evidence of when we have stopped moving is suicide. People who commit suicide feel they have nothing else to live for. The bitterness has taken root and loneliness soon follows. This place is found when there is no movement in the spiritual, body or mind; the epitome of the walking dead. Life has so much more to offer you when you come to an understanding that you must continue to move on. It is with this knowledge that life even becomes enjoyable. When you allow yourself to become stagnated, you open a door to become frustrated, depressed, fearful and angry at life. You then start to blame those around you because of the condition you have gotten yourself into. This is not a good state to experience for yourself nor is it for your loved ones that are around you. Cynical people (your "Haters") are born of this mindset, mocking friends and loved ones because of their success.

As it comes to the walking dead there is a good thing about it that you must know it does not happen overnight. This place of destruction has a process. Any time that you start to recognize the symptoms of non-movement, put forth every effort to keep moving before you become engulfed in it and lose control. Even in the darkest place of your mind, there is no place that the Word of God cannot penetrate and free you from.

Let me be clear and say, these challenges are not just tied to you.

"But remember that the temptations that come into your life are no different from what others experience.

> *And God is faithful. He will keep the temptation from*
> *becoming so strong that you can't stand up against it.*
> *When you are tempted, He will show you a way out so*
> *that you will not give in to it.*" (1 Corinthians 10:13 -
NKJV)

In this scripture, God is saying that whenever you get into a situation that pulls you in a direction you do not want to go in, He will **ALWAYS** open a door for you to escape. Because of the love that God has for us, there has not been a situation created that can defeat Him – this is His promise to us. Man's logic would say that a circumstance or situation may be too difficult to overcome, but that is why God's ways are different than the ways of man; they are as far as the heavens are from the earth.

The first sign of all sin begins with comfort. Where there is comfort, there can be no progression. The runner that wants to run faster cannot go at a pace that is comfortable to him. He must push himself in order to increase his speed or he must push his stamina to run farther distances. To move is to never remain in the same place OR in the same position. It is to constantly and consistently push yourself to greater heights in God. To not allow what broke you yesterday to break you today. To not allow what depressed me yesterday to have the same stronghold on me that it did yesterday.

When something is not moving that has the capacity to move, it is either incapable because it is paralyzed or it is incapable because it is dead. It is better for us if we are paralyzed for a period of time in our spiritual movement, rather than be dead in our spirits. If we are paralyzed within our spirits, then movement can start again with time and work. However, time will not heal that which is dead. You have heard the question, "what happens when an unstoppable force meets an immovable object?" Well, what does happen? God is the unstoppable force and when we become stagnated in our walk, we become the immovable object. Who is it that can resist God's will? When we stop moving, we come against a force that does not intend on us resting until we move according to His purpose. So you see, any kind of movement does not release you, but at least it can steer you back on course; however, that which does not move cannot be steered in any direction.

God uses trials and tribulations to get us to move. Movement in God brings peace.

> *"Therefore, having been justified by faith, we have peace with God through our Lord Jesus Christ, through whom also we have access by faith into his grace in which we stand, and rejoice in hope of the glory of God. And not only that, but we also glory in the tribulations, knowing that tribulation produces perseverance; and perseverance, character; and character hope. Now hope does not disappoint, because the love of God has been poured out in our hearts by the Holy Spirit, who was given to us."* *(Romans 5:1-5)*

Do not allow people to say to you that if you are moving in God there will be no trials in your life and life will be a peaceful journey without the problems. That simply is not how our Heavenly Father operates. When you face obstacles in your life then count it all as joy.

The trials were meant to move you along to your purpose, not to bring so much fear to you that they paralyzed you. If something stays paralyzed for too long a period of time, then its muscles will start to deteriorate and things that may not have had the power to defeat them before will begin to feed off of them. This is the importance of us to "Keep It Moving".

Do not sit and cry about your situation because it shows that you have given up or on the brink of giving up. For instance, if someone in your life dies, do not shed tears because of death. Death to us means "no more", but death to Christ means "sleep". You are crying about a situation that in your mind is dead, but through the power of God, everything can be regenerated. Shed tears because you will miss them for a time, but don't shed tears because it is over... it is not over until God says it's over. Don't give up, keep moving.

I say to husbands, "Don't give up, because that praying wife gives you strength. ***Keep It Moving.***" Some of you reading this book are afraid that the bank is about to take your house, but the bank can't take your house because a believer is in it! ***"Keep It Moving..."*** You may even be worried about your job that just laid you off, but instead you ought to thank God for the promotion. In case you have not figured it out yet, "faith" is motion. Faith will keep you moving, and the lack of faith will cause you to be immovable or stagnate.

Breaking New Ground is to get your mindset ready, but continuing to **"Keep It Moving"**, is to awaken your faith! It is faith that connects you to God, not just wanting faith, but faith in action!

In the process of moving with God you find yourself. And in finding out about yourself, you find out more about God. So, trust God with every movement you make, and it will be impossible to go wrong. If you move with a Godly plan or a Godly direction, there will always be a righteous end.

Remember that the only way you can move forward, is to release and forget the past in your life. Otherwise, instead of moving forward to the future, you will move back with the past.

Reflection

1. Are you comfortable living at your current level?

2. Do you have friends who want to see you stay at the same level? Reflect on the reasons they may want you to stay there.

3. Is there anyone that pushes you to move forward in life?

4. Are you willing to trust God with the trials that are intended to keep you moving?

Don't quite know how or what to do to form a relationship with God? Email me at: livingfree@authorshippublishing.com

Keep It Moving

Reader's Notes

_____

_____

_____

_____

_____

_____

_____

_____

_____

_____

_____

_____

_____

_____

_____

_____

_____

_____

_____

_____

_____

_____

_____

_____

_____

_____

_____

Liberating Yourself

One of the most challenging tasks you will ever have to experience is liberating yourself. This task is difficult because it requires a great deal of effort and self-control on one's own part. Why is there so much self-control and effort that must be demonstrated? This is because it means that you have to remove the dead weight from yourself. Dead weight may be many years of built up guilt and shame. Dead weight can also be taking on the opinions of others as well as our own personal criticisms of ourselves. All of this weight pollutes our spirits. Be aware that personal criticisms of yourself are even more toxic than the opinions of others. How you see yourself goes deeper into your spirit and when it has become rooted in your spirit, it starts to manifest itself through your actions. This is when the illusion starts to take the form of reality. At this point, we start acting out and making visible the pain that is within (which was an illusion), then the struggle to get out of you what is destroying the image of you must happen. This is all happening at a sub-conscience level, which means you do not know you are acting in such a way in front of others. The Bible tells us that whatever is in us must come out of us, this includes the illusion we have formed into reality.

Allow me to be very candid and personal in this section because when I speak of having to liberate yourself from anything, I am implying that you are a slave to it. If there is anything that can stop you from moving, you will have to liberate yourself from it. What exactly are we liberating ourselves from, you may ask. We can sit and discuss all the devil talk we would like, but our minds really cannot fathom an entity that wants to doom us. Most of us think of Satan as a red thing with horns coming out of its head and a tail. We can barely comprehend the natural, so I will not spend so much time in this book on the supernatural.

When I speak of liberating yourself, I am speaking of releasing yourself from what people say or think of you. It is the poison that chokes out many people's faith. We may pretend that we do not care about what people think, but allow me to prove to you just how much we care. Many of us, even if we don't want to, stay in the latest styles with everything the world has to offer. We want the BMW, Mercedes, and Lexus. Have you ever asked yourself why you really wanted to drive these cars? People have made these cars a sign of financial stature. We know that when others see us in these cars they automatically give us the praises that come along with having such an expensive automobile. We have allowed what people think to govern what we also want out of life.

Another example is when you see a beautiful man or woman walking down the street you meet and converse with and soon find out each other is interesting, and you instantly want to date this person. After the second date, the person tells you that they are actually a prostitute, but they want to give it up for you. They tell you that they want to meet your friends and family. What is it that you would immediately start thinking, "What are my friends and family going to think?" At that moment you would have forgotten about the happiness of what you felt for that person, and you would then start to see and view them as your family and friends would view them; concerned about what they would say, think or feel.

Even in marriages we do not live with freedom. Before we get married, we try everything out in the bedroom we possibly can, and usually when we are doing these things, we are doing it with someone whose opinion we don't care about. We don't care if they think we are a freak or not, we just want our sexual pleasure the way we want it. However, when we are married we retire that behavior because we are too afraid of what our spouse may think of us. We don't want to put the cheerleader outfit on. We don't want to be erotic with our spouses because we are too afraid that they may think less of us. If there is anyone you should be free to please, it is your spouse. Some of our spouses will ask us to do these things and we would deny them and then go cheat on them and do that same thing our spouse asked us to do to the person we are cheating with. I can't speak for everyone, but my wife and I don't mind pulling over on the side of the road when we are traveling. We are free. Free from what the world calls standards and appropriate, to be free in God.

One of the things that tend to destroy churches is the fact that we can't worship God like He wants us to because we're too busy worrying about what other people think. However, in God there is freedom, there is liberation. If you are not free in God, then you are enslaved to man and his opinions of you. Certainly, I am not saying that you are not accountable to people, but following God and being free in God allows you the opportunity to please God and to please the majority of people (it is much easier to please God than it is to please people). By being a man of God and doing what God commands of me, allows me to also be a better husband to my wife and to please her. Because I am commanded by God to not commit adultery, then it boosts the confidence in my wife, so she can be free with what the Lord has for her to do instead of worrying about what I am doing when I am away from her. There is freedom; the freedom to serve. Liberation liberates, so you not only free yourself but those who are around you are also freed.

Many of God's people or just people in general wrestle with the fact that they can never truly be themselves because of the layers of pain embedded inside. We live a lifetime not realizing the potential inside of ourselves, and that is not the will of God. The question becomes "How do I liberate myself so that I may become all God intended me to be in this life?"

Liberation is a mindset. It is when an individual takes an examination of one's own self. Being liberated will bring you out of the dark shadows in your life, and awaken you to things you had not seen before. It is those shadows that confine you to the prison of internal darkness, and *this* could destroy the will of the most powerful men or women. The process of liberation is not an overnight process. It will take a strong will, tears, and time to uncover your internal challenges. This is why it is of the utmost importance that we seek to liberate ourselves. Someone would say it is up to God to liberate us. In other words, what they're saying is that we don't have to do any work. Ignore these people, for that is why so many new found Christians become stagnated.

It is liberation that frees us to advance to other spiritual levels. An example of this is the moment your confidence level becomes greater as a result of

27

you not having anything to hang over your head *(your secrets)*. You are able to speak with authority, for you know that man can no longer give his opinion of you and cause you to doubt yourself. When you have no guilt trip (secrets) to wrestle with, you become a force. You see the first strategy of the devil is to show you your past, so he can hold you back and hold you down. Those being used by the devil will attempt to remind you of just how bad you were in the past. Stay in your confidence level because with confidence comes encouragement, followed by understanding, and eventually, the peace of mind sets in of who you are. It is at this point that you stop worrying about your life. With this realization, you stop wasting energy on how your life will end up, start depending on God and come into a place of liberty.

> *"Where the Spirit of the Lord is there is liberty."(2 Corinthians 3:17 -NKJV)*

So when you walk with God, which is the Spirit, then also walk in liberty. Liberty comes from the word "liberate". When you liberate yourself, you walk in freedom. Walking in freedom allows you to live your life separated from condemnation and opinions of others.

The greatest thing about liberating yourself is that now you have the ability to liberate others. Every person would love to live a life freed from the oppression of their past, this is called "ministry". You don't have to be a licensed minister to minister. Ministers talk to others about the freedom that is found in the Word of God. The Spirit within you, your lifestyle, and your walk with God both separately and collectively will cause others to want to pattern their lives after yours. I am a firm believer that you can only get the best out of people when they are liberated.

One of the great things about being liberated is that it will be hard to have pride, hard to be jealous, hard be hateful, hard to be envious and hard to be selfish. When one has become liberated it is like a light is shining over their soul, exposing it and guarding it from all the shadows of negativity in life. Shadows cannot exist in light, for light exposes everything. This light will help you to notice when your personality begins to change. When your personality starts to regress, it means that something is trying to take your freedom from you. Being liberated is a positive way of saying that, *"I choose to live a good life. I choose to be successful. I choose to be prosperous."* This is the type of attitude that bellows out, *"I will not be denied!!"* You have begun to take control of your life and truly believe that there is nothing impossible when God is on your side. Liberate yourself for success!

Reflection

1. Identify the dead weight that needs to be removed from your life.

2. What are some outside criticisms that you have attached to your identity?

3. Is there anything in your life that hinders you from worshipping God?

Don't quite know how or what to do to form a relationship with God? Email me at: *livingfree@authorshippublishing.com*

Liberating Yourself

Reader's Notes

_____

_____

_____

_____

_____

_____

_____

_____

_____

_____

_____

_____

Darrell Summerville

Liberating Yourself

32

I Am Gifted

What is a gift? A gift is something someone gives you as a token of appreciation for the things you have done. A gift can be given as a result of the love that someone has for you. Gifts are also given as an indication of friendship. A true gift is something given freely, meaning given without any strings attached. So many times we give a gift looking for something in return, but this is not what the meaning of "gift" was intended to be. Giving something and expecting something in return is called an exchange.

We give gifts to brighten someone's day or to lighten someone's load. God intended for a gift to be a supernatural way of saying "You don't have to struggle for this. I give it freely and you may freely receive it." A gift given in its true form could change the course of someone's life. We must be careful of how and what we give because we can destroy someone's spirit with wrong intentions or a wrong frame of mind. Giving with the wrong intent and a wrong frame of mind will create a negative image of yourself that could follow you through life.

The greatest gift ever given was God giving His only begotten son, Jesus, to die for our sins. A man with no sin died for the sins of others. What greater love could someone do than to give his only son's life so that others may have a chance at life? God didn't have to do it, but He did it to show His love for us. Jesus, being the gift for you and me, sacrificed His life in glory and came down from glory and gave his life on earth so that we may live free from sin. Jesus is the example of the power of a gift, which can change lives forever.

If Jesus was a gift for me, this makes me a gift to others. If I am a gift to others this means I am also gifted. To be gifted means that I have the power to brighten your day or lighten your load. God has placed gifts inside of you so that you may be a blessing to someone else.

In addition to the previously mentioned gift with Christ, God has given us the gift of love. This gift was not given to us just for us to love ourselves, or those whom we are fond of. Don't get me wrong, there is nothing wrong with loving yourself, but a gift is intended to be shared or given to others. The gift of love brings people closer to God. The gift of love from God is so powerful that we can't explain what love is; we can only show what it is. When God loves through us, we allow this love to pull others to God and not ourselves.

The next gift is one more powerful than knowledge and wisdom, it is the gift of understanding. Many people withdraw within themselves because they are misunderstood. If you have the gift of understanding you are able to relate to that person's soul. You have the ability to understand where that person is in life and you are able to bring them out of their withdrawal. Those gifted with understanding means that you must be gifted at listening. Understanding brings forth knowledge of a situation and the gift of understanding is given to help someone else know what they are going through.

There is also the gift of peace. When a person's life is in the state of chaos or *ungodliness*, the gift of peace will calm their spirit so they can think and gather themselves. Peace is an external gift that must be given, it cannot come from within. Human nature does not allow peace to be something that a person is able to create or share; we can only accept it or enjoy it. The Holy Spirit is the outside entity that brings into our lives the gift of peace.

The gift of joy is the one that we use most often. A person with the gift of joy can walk into a depressed situation and give an individual the ability to look at their situation and know that it is not the end of the world. Joy inspires hope within them; the very hope that their situation can change.

True gifts are not a physical aspect, but a spiritual item. You cannot see your physical body as a gift to someone, and it be truly a gift; there must be an association with the physical. If a woman believes her gift is her vagina then that is the thing that she will guard or give when she is ready to give her "gift". However, the vagina or any physical part of a person's body can never be declared a gift from God. Television encourages us to believe that the way a person may look or the way a person may move is a gift, but those things are not gifts.

A gift that was given to mankind that we can all take comfort in is the gift of the Holy Spirit. Christ ascended into Heaven but before He left, He said that he would send us a comforter, and that comforter is the Holy Spirit.

> *"But the Comforter, which is the Holy Ghost, whom*
> *the Father will send in my name, he shall teach you*
> *all things and bring all things to your remembrance*
> *whatsoever I have said unto you.." (John 14:26 –*
> *KJV)*

The Holy Spirit is part of the Trinity, which is the Father, the Son, and the Holy Spirit. You may wonder why this Comforter was sent. God sent the Comforter because He knew that it would be difficult to live this life without help. He sent us the Holy Spirit in order to teach us how to walk in this life.

The Holy Spirit is the "thing" that gives us the secrets of Heaven, for no one knows what Heaven is like, but it is the Holy Spirit that gives us a glimpse of what is happening. The Holy Spirit is the spokesman for God, and it is the search light that shines over my soul. The darker it is, the stronger it shines. It reveals what is good for us and what is bad for us. Yes, it is the "vibe" I feel that lets me know those people who are not good for me.

The Holy Spirit gives us power over all of our situations and makes us supernatural beings. It is the influence to go on when we feel like giving up. It helps us to understand who God is and how God moves. It is the Holy Spirit that can look into our future and tell us everything that looks good. A comforter would not be a comforter if it did not encourage us and allow us to trust and believe that we can make it. The Holy Spirit is a preparatory, it prepares for the thing that God is getting ready to do.

In our lives, we may see things happening and we are unable to understand what's going on, it is the Holy Spirit preparing us for what God has already said is coming. In this capacity, it knows when to get you ready and when it is the right time to prepare you because God is a timely god.

Many ask, "Well how do I obtain the Holy Spirit?" Let me tell you this: The Holy Spirit is a gift and you must be born again in order to receive it. You must live a life that is separated from sin. We cannot freely sin and expect to receive such a profound gift. If we separate ourselves from sin it sees this clean temple (your body) and takes up residency there. The Holy Spirit cannot dwell in an unclean temple, so you will not be able to live an unclean life and expect it to come in. It brings with it a sign that says "Owner Occupied" and it means that this temple is for God's use only.

The gifts that God has given us are not for any personal gain, but to help others when they are in a time of need. Some of us don't give out our gifts because we feel inadequate in doing so, and if we feel we are inadequate we feel that our gift is inadequate as well. Truth be told, no one wants to give a gift in which they feel is inadequate.

God has equipped us with every resource we need to be successful in this life; we just need to recognize our gifts and abilities. You may ask yourself, "How do I know what I am gifted to do?" You are gifted to do whatever it is that gives you peace; the things that you are naturally good at doing. All of these things are an indication of the things that you are gifted to do.

You may already know that gifts are not always used in a positive manner. Some people are very gifted and often use their gifts in negative ways. For example, a drug dealer may have the gift of being prosperous in whatever he does, but with that same gift, he could be prosperous selling cars. In addition, a prostitute that sells her body night and day can use that same gift of perseverance to sell real estate. These examples are gifts that could be used in a positive and negative way. We must understand that it is God who gives gifts, but how we use them is what makes the difference.

> *"For the gifts and callings of God are without repentance."* (Romans 11:29 - KJV)

This scripture means that God has no respect of a person, whether you are a practicing believer or not. God gives us gifts so we can function as a complete human being in this life. This is why it is important that you understand who you are in God and understand what gifts you have and how they function.

The wonderful aspect of God is that He is a just God. He gives us a life that we can appreciate or a life of shame; it's your choice. God's free will to us allows us to come to Him with a pure heart. God will not force us to do anything against our will. It is possible to live a free and gifted life in our Savior Christ Jesus. Know what you are gifted to do.

Reflection

1. Reflect on the state of your life today. Have you accepted who you are, or are you still afraid of truly discovering yourself?

2. List 3 to 5 things (talents/hobbies/abilities) that you feel that you are naturally good at.

3. List 3 to 5 things (talents/hobbies/abilities) that bring peace to your life.

4. Have you used the lists in items number 2 and 3 to glorify God? List 3 to 5 ways that you can use these gifts to glorify God?

If you have not accepted the Lord Jesus Christ as your personal Savior and would like to speak to someone, feel free to contact me at:
livingfree@authorshippublishing.com

I Am Gifted

Reader's Notes

_____

_____

_____

_____

_____

_____

_____

_____

_____

_____

_____

_____

I Have To Win This Battle

"Battle" is a term most often used when we are going through a conflict with some type of opposing force. We all have experienced different battles daily. Some of these battles are quick and easy while others are long and exhaustive.

The daily battles we face are both external and internal. External battles exist when you are fighting off any individual or entity that tries to tear you down. These are battles that form when there is stress on the job, when friends walk away from you, when friends are talking about you and financial difficulties arise - these are the very struggles in life that we all face. Typically, we do not prepare ourselves for these battles, but we must. They will come because they are needed in order to help build your awareness. Awareness is something that is mandatory in order to progress because you will never know when life is getting ready to throw you a curve ball.

In order to survive these external battles you must be prepared for the struggle. Life, by its very design, is a struggle and may seem to be unfair; however, what may be unfair to you may be fair to someone else. "C'est la vie" and life evolves, for it changes and it turns. When it seems that things are not going your way, it is just time for you to win some battles.

God allows battles to come to make us stronger and no person really wants to lose a battle. So your battle cry going into the battle must be "I must win this battle!", and when you grasp this understanding, the battle becomes only a frame of mind. If you can win a battle within your mind (which is where external battles are truly fought), you have also won the physical battle. It is a learning process of victory that can be controlled by you.

The second type of battle that you must win is the internal battles. Internal battles are much greater than the external battles. This is a battle that we have with ourselves. If one does not know his own strengths and weaknesses, the battle forces him to another level in your life - give ground or take ground. There are so many types of internal battles, but some of the common or familiar ones are:

> ➤ **Low self esteem**
> ➤ **Lack of Confidence**
> ➤ **Insecurity**
> ➤ **Fear**

Low self esteem *can be defined as not having respect for yourself, a feeling of worthlessness; it is to never feel good enough in comparison to others; feeling unworthy of anything positive or good; the lack of confidence; being insecure.*

The key to victory over the battle of low self esteem is to never say what you cannot do, and you will find yourself winning easily by just doing it. Even if you fail, you can at least have peace within yourself knowing that you had the power to try, and that is good enough.

Lack of Confidence *is really a lack of faith, while confidence can be defined as having little or no doubt in your ability or talent to achieve.*

Confidence is simply the belief in one's self. Confidence in one area brings confidence in other areas. When you apply or assert confidence, you simply are taking something that makes you uncomfortable and doing it until you get it right.

Insecurity *can be defined as not having confidence or having little or no self esteem.*

The key to victory over the battle of insecurity is to never allow negativity to get into your spirit and then settle. If you allow this process to begin, it will have you looking at everything else in a negative way.

Fear *can be defined as the absence of faith; being afraid or scared of what might happen. Fear is a "future factor" – not knowing the future or being unsure of a future outcome.*

This internal battle has the power to paralyze you. The key to victory over fear is to not let low self esteem, lack of confidence, and insecurity to take root. These three internal battles cause fear.

When you give your life to God then you also are saying to God that this battle is not my own to win but His. This is exactly what God wants us to do... Win.

The spouse that is unfaithful to you was not meant for you to fight with, but to allow God to step in and conquer. The boss at work that provokes you so he can fire you is not your battle. Ask God to come in and rescue you, and believe in your heart that He can do it.

My dear sisters and brothers, God equips us for battle, it is when we walk into battle alone that we are ill-equipped. I know of someone who said that their boss at their job was giving them a hard time and so one day they yelled at the boss and quit. That person went on to tell me that it must be God's will for this to have happened to them. But, how can God fight for us if we are in the way fighting? He waits until we see we are no match for the obstacle and it is at that time that He moves to conquer all. By Him working through us and for us in such a way, we become more than conquerors as well.

To someone who is not a Christian that is reading this, it may seem like rubbish to stop fighting and trust that an unseen force will fight a battle for him. Most of us have never seen the President of the United Sates in person; we've only had the television, the radio, or the words of other people to go by. Though we have never met the President, we trust that he is fighting battles for us in the White House so we may sleep peaceful at night.

New Christians that walk in the faith have a tendency to believe that once they come to God, this walk is without challenges. Not only is the walk of faith filled with obstacles, but one must be humble and a warrior at the same time. We must be fearful to go out of the will of God and fearless to go where God leads us.

The boss at the job that is looking for a reason to fire you has already been defeated. You just have to endure and be ready when you are called upon. Not to feel personally attacked, but to know that the war that you are a part of is not a personal battle. It is the enemy's goal to have you to think that you are alone and without aide, without hope and without a chance to win. No man is an island.

The key to conquering the battle is to first realize that you have a power that resides within you that cannot be conquered. This power does not know what it means to retreat or to be defeated. If it was God that gave you the job, then only God can take it away from you. Your boss cannot do anything to you that God does not allow. Being fired in the eyes of man sometimes means getting a promotion in God's!

We have been misled to think that this battle is for things that are materialistic in nature. We have become fearful of losing our homes, cars, status in society and even our lives. All of these things were given to us by God as gifts, and it is He who decides when they will be no more or if we will have more. God only requires a willing vessel and it is He that takes care of the rest.

The internal and external battles will strengthen you so when they come upon you, look to the Lord and dare Him to rescue you. When the trials come, stand firm on His word; He said He would never leave us or forsake us. You just have to believe it. When your enemies try to tear you down, do not react or give evil for evil. Pray for your enemies and stand with humility, for that will be like throwing heaps of hot coals on their heads.

There once was a man that was lying in his bed and one night he heard the voice of God say to him, *"Michael, I have placed a large boulder outside your door. Every morning I want you to rise and push against the boulder. I am the God that you serve and my strength is within you."* The man knowing that he had just heard a word from God was excited and morning came to him in a matter of minutes. As God commanded Michael, he went outside and as God had said to him in the dream, there was a huge boulder outside the door. The man placed his hands against the boulder and started pushing with all of his strength. He pushed the boulder that morning until evening. This went on for several weeks, Michael pushing against the boulder with all of his strength. The man's faith and obedience had gotten the attention of Satan and one night Satan went to visit him. He said to the man, "Michael, I have watched you push against the boulder outside your door everyday as you were commanded, but this task you were given is impossible. Your neighbors and family see you as crazy and rightly so. You have been pushing that boulder for weeks and yet you have not moved it even an inch. Every day you have pushed against it with all of your strength, and you have achieved nothing. You will say that God told you to do this, but are you sure?"

The man began to then start thinking of what Satan said to him and he became saddened. He realized that he had not moved the boulder and he had alienated his friends and family. Michael began to feel tired and right when he was ready to quit, he decided to pray to God. He said to God "Lord, I love you and I don't know why you have asked me to do something that I am not able to do. I have pushed the boulder outside for weeks and have not moved it one inch. I want to quit but before I do, did you speak to me?"

God heard the man and responded to him, *"Michael, you have done what I have asked you to do, but you forgot what I told you. I commanded you to push against the boulder, not to move the boulder. Now look at your hands, see how they have grown rugged and strong. Look at your chest and back; see how they have become chiseled like granite. Look at your legs; see how they are strong like roots of an old tree. I have made you strong so you can go out and lead those men I will put in your charge. You are obedient to me but I need you to look strong for these men, for you must look stronger than them in their eyes. Pushing against the boulder was to teach you patience, which is what you will need when you become a leader of men. When trials come your way then I would have already prepared you to keep pushing onward, even if you are unable to see the progress you have made. By pushing against the boulder I have taught you commitment, to stay committed to my work even when those around you start becoming uncommitted to you. I was getting you prepared for my will. Who then has come in and poisoned your thoughts?"*

This story is to point out that we have been called to get ready for battle and God calls us to keep pushing. If you can't see Him moving, that's OK, just keep on pushing because he uses our trials to make us stronger to lead us while we are in this battle.

We must understand that these battles must be won because they are steps that take you to the next level. No one minds going into battle if they know they are going to win. The scriptures tell us we can win if we put our trust in God.

> *"The weapons of our warfare are not carnal but*
> *mighty through God..." (2 Corinthians 10:4)*

This verse is telling us not to waste time over things that will not benefit us. We go into battle for the things that God has already given to us, such as peace of mind or the support of our family. In picking your battles you should only undertake a battle in the things that will reward you in your purpose in life and not the things that hold you back. You should pick wisely because you cannot allow one battle to engulf you and drain you of all your energy.

Every battle is timely and comes at the time that has been predestined. While you are battling, make sure that the battle you are in builds your spirit and do not allow it to break you because it could consume your spirit. Never go through a battle, unless you have a Godly understanding of why you are in the battle.

It is equally important that you never go through a battle that you caused on your own because this only produces wasted time and effort. Fight with all of your might and emotion because these battles are taking you toward your destiny in life. The reason you cannot give up in the battle is because this means that you have to start all over again and continue with the battle process until you are the victor. It is true that the longer you battle, the longer you have to wait to reach your destiny, so don't stay in one battle for too long.

When you are in the battle ensure that you are in control of the battle and don't let the battle control you. You will find the battle dictating to you and this is where you may find yourself twirling out of control. After each battle, take the time to review your keys to victory and how successful you were.

Remember, there are others going through the same battles as you, teach them how to win their battles. Teaching others to win a battle is just like giving them a million dollars, when you are able to teach others it promotes you to a different level in life. As you can see, it is not just your life that hangs in the balance, but the lives of others as well. Remember your battle cry, **"I Have To Win This Battle!"**

Reflection

1. Identify the external battles that have been repeating themselves in your life.

2. What are some internal battles that you struggle with daily?

3. What does the chapter reveal about preparing for battle?

4. What is your main weapon against the battles you experience in life?

5. List 3 battle cries that will encourage you in the face of the battle.

If you have not accepted the Lord Jesus Christ as your personal Savior and would like to speak to someone, feel free to contact me at:
livingfree@authorshippublishing.com

I Have To Win This Battle

Reader's Notes

_____

_____

_____

_____

_____

_____

_____

_____

_____

_____

_____

_____

_____

Watch How You Walk

When we are referring to the word "walk" we are using it in the context of lifestyle. Your walk (your lifestyle) tells a lot about you. It is the surest sign for others to know how you live without verbally expressing who and what you believe. What's excellent about this walk in Christ is that God gives us the ability to be anything we want to be as long as we are being ourselves.

God created us in His image and likeness, meaning that we have the characteristics and personality of God. If God is peculiar then that makes us peculiar people. Peculiar people are more often creative individuals and with this creativity come honor and respect.

Your walk must be filled with integrity, for one of God's traits is integrity. Integrity is not needed if we are only dealing with ourselves, but it is required when we are dealing with others. This means that your walk is really not for you, but for the glory of God. For that reason alone, it helps us walk upright since we know intimately that we are representing the Almighty.

As people of God we must come to understand that it is His life that is lived through us and not our lives lived through ourselves. Living through ourselves will ultimately bring failure, but God living through us makes us successful in all things that are in His will. This is the concept that connects the Godly and the ungodly, for we all want success. We all want to be able to say, "This is who I am." However, it is your walk that determines and expresses who you are. Your walk must align with your talk. Is it possible for a man's head to go in one direction while his feet travel in a different direction? No. Then it is also impossible for a Godly person to say one thing when your Godly walk is going in a different direction. This will cause confusion, not just for you, but for others that are watching your walk!

The reason why it is of the utmost importance to watch how you walk is because until another person discovers who they are in God, you will be the example of God they look to. There is always someone imitating your walk, and you are accountable for the direction in which you lead them... be careful. If you lead someone in the wrong direction, whether intentional or unintentional, their blood will be on your hands and you are accountable to the Lord. The good thing about a good walk is that if your life lines up with the word of God, then there is no way you can veer off course and lead someone in the wrong direction.

The word of God is a tool used for alignment, correction, and organization for us all. It automatically shows you how to align the feet with the mouth. So powerful is the word of God that regardless of the way it is exposed, either spoken or seen in a lifestyle, it changes the atmosphere.

A Lifestyle of Faith

Why is the walk of faith so important?

"For we walk by faith, not sight...." (2 Corinthians 5:7-KJV)

God looks for total trust in Him because walking by faith pleases God in all measures, through all times. Total faith in God means you have totally submitted to Him. When we have submitted to Him, then it is only our faith that moves us out of the way. When we are in full submission, we allow God to perform His Blessing on our lives. God is faithful, but He is only made faithful to His word. If your lifestyle is according to the word of God, then it has to do what you are asking it to do, because you are only asking it to do what God has given you the authority to do.

This authority can also easily lead you in the wrong direction simply because of "you". Do not allow your walk to be tainted by your own wisdom or the wisdom of others. What I mean is while God is blessing you, don't try to figure out how He is doing it or let others misguide you in how He will do it. Because of the mind of mankind, our own will to figure things out brings about confusion, and confusion is not of God. It is impossible for God to work against Himself. He will not speak something to you and then leave you confused. It is always us that bring in the confusion into our lives.

You wonder, *"How do I know if it is God's words or man's wisdom?"* You will know it is God's words because you will have peace in your spirit. The spirit of God will agree with the word of God in what you are asking.

To walk in the flesh or in your own understanding disconnects you from God because God recognizes faith and is called to it. When you are connected to God you can hear Him and recognize his voice because there is peace. You, at that time, will hear what He is saying, and then you are able to hear what He is thinking because the Holy Spirit seeks out what is good for your life and warns you of those things that could disconnect you from God.

My dear friend, **faith is not what you have, it is who you are**. When I use faith as what "I am" it brings me what I need. I do not get blessed from God because I have faith; I am blessed from God because I am faith, and I live in faith. Therefore, my walk is faith.

When God sees us He sees us through faith. God doesn't see me coming; He sees a faith named "Darrell" coming. In the scripture there was a woman who could not stop bleeding. Christ was in a crowd of people who wanted something, they were all touching him, but when faith touched him, he was able to recognize it because faith calls out for God's attention and energy.

Life's struggles will attempt to get you to walk away from God, but your faith is what will keep you connected to the Lord. My faith in God builds my relationship with God. It is simply not enough to know of God, but you must have an intimate relationship with Him. When God moves, you move. When God feels, you feel. God wants to walk and talk with His people. However, is there anyone who will take the time to diligently seek Him? When you diligently seek after Him, He opens up the Heavens and shows you the mysteries of Himself. The Maker has so much to say, but who will listen? Our spirits must be clean to hear Him and that is a daily walk. There are so many that say that they hear from God (and people follow them), but God only speaks through a pure and clean spirit. If someone says they hear from the Lord, check out their lifestyle with God. The scripture says for us to check the spirit by the spirit and see if it is of God.

God will not make Himself out to be ignorant or fallible. If God speaks through an individual, it will be confirmed by the scriptures. When God speaks, He speaks what He has already said in the Word. In other words, God doesn't come off the cuff just to please you. Those of you who seek after prophets to prophesy to you, please listen: If everybody says they hear from God (verbally) then there would be no reason to seek after God (in the scripture). The word tells us that:

> "...For many are called but few are chosen..."
> (Matthew 20:16 - KJV)

Everyone who says, "The Lord said..." may not be a vessel used to bring you closer to God.

Watch how you walk and how those that feed you spiritually walk. Make sure that what you say and what you say to others is actually from the Lord. If it is not, then you will be accountable for every incorrect and negative word you speak. Walk a good walk and live a good life so that when others see your lifestyle that it will glorify your Father which is in Heaven.

Understand that this walk, this life, this journey, is not about us; it is about others. When I think of all the young people today who do not believe in God, it saddens me deeply. They do not turn away from God or reject religion because of their own spiritual experience, but because they were watching how some other believer walked. It was at that point and time that they made a conscious decision not to be like the one they saw walking before them. This is the danger in not constantly monitoring your walk. By this I do not mean to become hypocrites because you cannot keep up a facade forever, sooner or later people will see who you are. You cannot fool people all the time. We all are discovered in our condition, to think you are fooling someone you are actually only fooling yourself.

There is an old gospel song called "I've Got a New Walk," which symbolizes the transformation of the Old Person to the New Person.

There are three walks that we will discuss:

> ➢   The walk of love.
> ➢   The walk of light.
> ➢   The walk of wisdom.

We are to walk in **love,** be imitators of Christ. When Jesus walked this Earth, He walked in love. This is how we too should walk. Not meeting people grudgingly, but greeting them with warmth and kindness. We can say a kind word to them to encourage when they are in need.

Love has a confident walk, for it knows that it is the most cherished gift that has ever been created. There will be those that see you walking and hate the fact that you walk so gracefully while exuberating confidence and strength. They will wonder where your strength comes from, not understanding that you are directly connected to God and positioned to succeed. It is the sweet smelling aroma of obedience that signifies your walk. The walk of love is the most substantial part of your Christian walk that you will come into, but it is not the only one.

We are to walk in **light.** Though we may have once been in the darkness of the enemy, we are awakened to the light which is the knowledge of the truth. As you know, light does not hide or conceal. In fact, light exposes all. It not only exposes those things that were once concealed, it also awakens those things that were once asleep.

Imagine if you will, this world being dark because the Lord has given it over to evil for a while. If you have ever been in a forest at night, then you know it is possible to see a small light from a far distance. Now imagine that the Lord has allowed His light to shine in you, it would then be possible for all the creatures of the darkness to see your light. This is how it works when our light shines for God. This is also why it is so easy for evil to sniff you out. As long as you are a light you will attract those things that are in the dark, but you will also be able to be a guide for those who have lost their way. How do you make your light shine brighter? The call to read your Bible in this walk is a necessity, but many who come into the faith overlook this. How can we know what is acceptable to God, unless you read His instructions to us? And how can we find peace and life if the way is not opened to us?

Walk in **wisdom.** The wise are insightful and they walk circumspectly, not as those that do not understand, but they walk as those with an understanding. They are always watching their paths to avoid contact with undesirable influences. For example, if you know you have a weakness with women, why would you put yourself in positions or places where you may be tempted? God gives us insight so that we may avoid snares and traps that have been laid for us by the enemy; the Bible even lists them for us.

The scripture tells us that there is nothing new under the sun. Therefore, there is nothing in which the wisdom of God cannot combat and defeat. To discern the will of God and to apply His wisdom is not a matter of your personal feelings or emotions, but of mental understanding. It is important to surround yourself with those who are able to offer wise counsel of God. To reject wise counsel is to reject God. One of the most important weapons you have at your disposal is those who are outside of your situation who may be able to offer life saving advice.

It is your walk that determines who is walking with you. By attraction, a liar walks with other liars, and the jealous walker brings other jealous spirits along with him. There is a positive result when you walk according to God's word that has already been foretold and promised to those that walk according to God's will. You may have stumbled in the beginning of your walk, but get up and start walking again is the key.

How you walk will define who you are because as you think it materializes in your walk. The ability to think cannot be done without a thought. What are your thoughts? How are you walking? The scripture says "so a man thinketh so is he." This is the importance of watching your thoughts because you alert people to what you are thinking by the speed or slowness in your walk. Before you move you have to think it through, even if it is not enjoyable.

Note to the Reader: This is the true "Secret", if you can gain nothing more from this entire book, be sure you gain the following. Since faith is the substance of things hoped for and the evidence of things not seen; it is impossible to see God with our naked eyes, so we must have faith to see Him. We wouldn't be able to feel Him or perceive Him without faith. Faith and doubt cannot coexist on the same plane or in the same space and time. Reader, do you know what you call people that have faith in everything? They are called 'rich'. Not just rich in money, but rich in everything. You will look at them and wonder why in a time of calamity or hardship that they welcome it and still have joy and success in these times. It is their faith that has made them this conqueror in all things. Your greatest walk in this life will be one that you don't see and you cannot see the outcome of. These ordered steps are the steps that require an exercise of your faith.

Reflection

1. Does your walk (lifestyle) represent a life of faith?

2. What could you adjust in your lifestyle to align your walk with that of Jesus Christ?

3. What steps can you take to incorporate the 3 walks (love, light, wisdom) into your life?

4. What is the true "secret" revealed in the chapter?

Watch How You Walk

Reader's Notes

_____

_____

_____

_____

_____

_____

_____

_____

_____

_____

_____

Don't Limit God

Contrary to popular belief, God is not in Heaven trying to develop a master plan on how to bless you. Would any entity with the absolute control of time and space need to develop a plan? Although He does not need to develop a plan, this does not mean that He does not have a plan for each and every one of us. He is marvelous and His concern is with us and how He may rescue us from ourselves. Since man works within time and his lifespan is measured in time, God must be timely in order to meet our needs and still not lose control. A perfect plan must have been laid from the beginning. The carpenter does not plan what the house will look like while he is building it, the plan is laid out before he even lifts a hammer.

To access our blessings takes praise and trust. There is no limit to what God can and will do for us; however, in order to believe these things you must come to an understanding of how great and splendid God really is. Man often fails because he limits God by knowing the limits of man. He fails to realize that God is limitless.

> *"Far as the Heavens are higher than the earth, so are my ways higher than your ways, and my thoughts higher than your thoughts." (Isaiah 55:9 - NKJV)*

This verse means that our minds cannot conceive the plans and paths God has for His people. In order for us to be used by the Lord, our minds will have to also stretch beyond our own comprehension to become omnipotent (all-powerful, authority, invincible, unstoppable or supreme). In other words, our earthly minds will never reach God's intellect. So what is it that connects us to God? What connects us to God is our faith. If you can just believe that God can do anything, then the Lord will take you to places that you would not believe. We are limited in our own understanding, but God has limitless understanding and it is His desire to bless us if we can only believe.

The death of Jesus set the wheels in motion for believers to live a life with "no limit". Before Christ died for our sins, we had to have someone intercede for us and take our needs to God because we were not worthy to stand in the presence of God. Jesus' death gave us the right to go to God for ourselves. We can now talk to God about how we are feeling. We can express our desires to Him. It is because of His love that He listens and comes to our rescue. The Lord desires to have an intimate relationship with His children.

> *"The eyes of your understanding being enlightened that you may know the hopes of His calling, and what the riches of the glory of His inheritance in the saints..."* *(Ephesians 1:18 – NKJV)*

The writer of this verse of scripture is not saying that we should open our physical eyes, but that we should open our spiritual eyes to the rich inheritance God has for His people. Once we can understand the exceedingly great power of God, then we can begin to understand that there are no limits to what God can and will do for us. Any limits we place on God holds us back from the inheritance that He has for us, therefore the limits we place upon Him must be removed.

We can live a lifetime beneath the privileges that God has for us when we use our own understanding. By limiting Him, we limit ourselves to know the greatness that God has placed within all of us. Faith moves us into a realm of expectation in God. With faith, you allow God to take you beyond your limits into a great destiny that has been waiting and calling out to you. The Lord has to push you out of your mind so that you can take on His mind in order to understand what you can be in this life. Take the limits off of God and live in a realm of possibilities where you can believe God for anything.

The call is to believe because you have to believe in order to receive the blessing coming. If God showed you what He had for you then it would be beyond your comprehension, so we must pray that God stretches our minds in order to believe. Most of the time, God will allow us to go to the end of our thought process, or to the end of what we can do, even to the end of our capabilities, before He begins His work. As long as we try to do it ourselves, we limit God's movements. If you look out of your own eyes you will only see what you are capable of doing, but when you can see out of God's eyes then you can see beyond your abilities and you start depending on God's capabilities. It is then that the possibilities of greatness start to open. By taking the limits off of God, you start to operate in a supernatural level of belief. This is the reason that when God blesses you, your mind can't conceive how it was done. This is our limited understanding at work. We are not supposed to understand how God did it; we are to just believe that He did and that He can do it again. Whoever God calls He can deliver what He expects out of them.

What I am about to say may be a little confusing, but please bear with me on what I am attempting to explain here. Mankind is limited in what we can do because mankind resides within space and time. We have to understand that time was created for us and not for God. We all get into a rush and feel pressured about certain situations we are in because of time. Time, by its very own design, puts constraints on everything that is within it. It is very important that you understand this point so please do not read further if you cannot.

Take for instance, a woman who is seeking to find a husband before her biological clock runs out. This urgency sometimes hampers her decision making process of who she should and should not be with. She could be a very beautiful woman that would not have given you the time of day when she is 25, but when time pressures her at the age of 35, you will see that her standards for a very suitable mate may drop considerably from what they once were. Pushed into a corner by the constraints of time, brings about rushing, which typically leads to bad decisions being made.

God, on the other hand, does not live within space and time. That is why the scriptures constantly echo that God does not change. He is the same God today, yesterday, and forever more. When we say God is the same, we are speaking literally and not figuratively. If the Lord hated a certain act of sin 5,000 years ago, then He hates the same act of sin today, for in His mind, time did not change. Furthermore, because He does not reside in space or time He has no constraints; He is free to be God.

Everything that lives within space and time has to change. There is nothing that remains the same, no, not even the Earth itself. God has no boundaries, so there is no change. Because time causes things to change, and He does not change, then His words cannot change. When David says...

> *"I have been young and now I am old, yet I have not seen the righteous forsaken nor his decedents begging for bread" (Psalms 37:25 – NKJV)*

David's words in this verse of scripture still holds true today.

If you are righteous in God's eyes, which is impossible to be in the eyes of people, then you cannot be forsaken, God will hear you. Many of us don't have the desires of our hearts because we do not claim it with faith. Faith without works is dead, and <u>faith without works is called "hope"</u>. Hope is the perception that what is wanted can be had, or that events will turn out for the best with us having to do little or no action.

A poor person financially hopes that he will become rich, but an heir to an estate claims his riches. We are heirs of Christ and we have the power to "name it and claim it". We do not hope that things will work out for the best for us, because God has already written that it shall. When we typically use the word "shall" we mean that we plan to, intend to, or expect to. However, when God uses the word "shall", He uses it as a contract that has been given into law and He means something must, is, or obliged to. When Christ says we have not because we ask not, it means that we suffer without because we have not taken the action to claim what is ours by law.

Mothers, you have a call to be righteous for your children's sake. Not only will God not forsake you in your time of need, but David says he has never seen a righteous person's seed begging bread either. When you live a righteous life, then it sets your children up as well for blessings. Why are the NBA and NFL receiving all of these people with poor backgrounds? It is because more than likely they had a praying mother that cried out to God. The power of a praying mother will always defy the laws of physics.

How many times have you not filled out a job application because you felt like you were not qualified? You probably missed out on your blessing because of it. Let me try to get you to understand something, righteous people command the attention of the world. I don't mean those Christians who talk loud and make a scene, I am referring to those who are silent in their righteousness. Once you say you are a child of God, then people put you in a box and they think they have you figured out. When they don't know what you believe, they think there is just something good or different about you. When you get their attention, then they feel the need to figure you out.

Do not be afraid of rejection because that means you are not trusting that God will do what He has already said He would do for you. When you come to trust in God then you come to understand that man can't hire and man can't fire you. The footsteps of the righteous are directed by God, so have faith and take the limits off of God.

We worship a limitless God and His expectations for your life are far beyond your understanding. And just because you do not understand it doesn't mean God won't do what He said He will do. It just means that the Lord is getting ready to take you to another level. God allows troubles to come into our lives, not to kill us, but to stretch our minds to believe. At that time you would not have depended on man, but on God. Take the limits off of Him and begin to live free!

Reflection

1. Are you living by faith or are you living by hope? Identify the difference between the two listed in the chapter.

2. What are some characteristics of a person that lives by faith? How can you adopt some of these characteristics into your life?

3. List the scriptures that are outlined in this chapter. Commit these verses to memory or post them in a visible place (mirror, car, refrigerator, etc.) to use when your faith seems to lessen.

Don't Limit God

Reader's Notes

_____

_____

_____

_____

_____

_____

_____

_____

_____

_____

_____

_____

Know Who You Are

To walk in this life it is quintessential that you know who you are. In contrast, not knowing who you are is like being a walking dead man/woman, a zombie if you will. God has given us an identity that is far beyond our understanding of ourselves. The plan was set even before the foundations were laid for the Earth. The relationship between the Lord and man had already been forged. We were all called sons and daughters of God. Like Melchizedek we were all part of a royal priesthood.

> *"But you are a chosen generation, a royal priesthood, a Holy nation, a peculiar people, that ye should shew forth the praise of Him who hath called you out of the darkness into the marvelous light."*
> *(1Peter2:9 - KJV)*

We were known as the children of light, chosen by God because every other nation had their own god. These gods were made by man out of gold and silver. They also worshiped animals because it was difficult for them to worship a god they could not see. They worshiped things they could relate to or what was of significance to them. The exchange was that their flesh was now satisfied. This was not just for those people in biblical times, but for us as well. We are not to worship material things or rely on them because then we would be promoting a creation such as cars, houses, money, jobs, or the loved ones of our lives to God.

The children of Israel were a people who refused to worship any other god, but the God 'Jehovah' which is the God of Isaac, Abraham, and Moses. Many names He may be called, but the omnipotence of this one entity is undeniable by any name. As long as Israel stayed with this God, Jehovah, they had an identity. Because we were made from God and in His likeness, to not know Him is to not know who you are. Once you know who you are, you understand your purpose, and identity is born from purpose. When we stay with God we have identity in our lives. And we can only recognize who we are with God.

So many say they are lost, or they are looking for themselves. This is indeed true when you have an identity crisis. Mankind lost its identity in the Garden of Eden with Adam and Eve. This was the fall of man, the separation of mankind from its purpose. Adam was given dominion over every living thing in the garden, but because of disobedience it caused us to lose who we are. It then became impossible for a faithful man to be a lost man, but disobedience erases faith and puts us all on the path to uncharted territory. This uncharted territory is the Law of Sin and shame, so God had to redeem us from these laws. To be made free and set us back in the right course, God sent his own son down from Heaven to die for our sins so we could regain our identities.

To know who you are is not just a blessing, but it is a miracle and a privilege. Depression cannot take root when we walk in authority and confidence. This may sound unbelievable, but it is true, when you know who you are you discover that you have God-like characteristics. The more you seek God, the more you become like God; you take on God's spirit. Therefore, it is that power that helps understand who you are in God.

Remember it is an exchange. Someone gave up their life so that you could have life. A mother delivering a baby during childbirth is as close to the example as one can get. She has to put her life on the line in order for the child to have life. No one who sacrifices their life for you does it so that you can emulate someone else, but it was done so you could be yourself... the "you" that God gave you purpose to be. It is so easy to be like the things we see day to day, and so hard to be yourself.

As a matter of fact, you can only be great when you're being yourself. No great writer, painter, or thinker was made great by imitating someone else they saw. These individuals were counted as "great" because they were perceived to be the first that ventured out of the norm to be great writers, painters, or thinkers. The nature of God is that He will only make you great while you are being yourself.

When God calls a leader out of the people, He calls him because He put greatness in that person. He calls him to be himself. This is why all good leaders help you bring out the best in yourself. The great thing about being called by God is to be able to speak power into someone's life. It is truly exciting. A person with greatness can see greatness in another, and this is why sometimes we don't really know what's in us until someone Godly tells us. Only a strong person can tell you that you are strong because only a person who knows who they are can tell you who you are. Never allow a weak person to define who you are... weak begets weak.

Knowing who you are helps you to become victorious over your circumstances. Without diligently seeking who God is, you cannot come to the conclusion of who you are. The more you know of God, the more you know of yourself. Because I am of God, it makes me a character inheritance of God. This makes me exceptional through Christ Jesus.

> *"Nay, in all these things we are more than conquerors through Him that loves us."* (Romans 8:37 - KJV)

We can face all challenges with the Lord on our side; for if the power of the universe is with me, who then can stand against me and succeed? With such absolute power, it takes an absolute mind and spirit.

God wants us to stop "feeling like" we know who He is and truly "know" who He is. In those times when you don't feel like a child of God, step outside of yourself and understand that pain spurts growth and the same is true in spiritual levels. When things are not going well you must still know who you are so that you may conquer the trial. A prince that does not know he is heir to the throne is a commoner.

God will allow uncomfortable things to happen in your life and then tell you to speak or walk with the authority of the King behind you so that you may go one step closer in discovering your true identity. Once you understand the power that flows through to you, then you will come to have a better understanding of your gifts from God. He does not want us walking around ignorant of what He is doing in our lives. The Lord wants you to know so that you can give Him the glory. If you ever think you are actually doing it yourself, then you have lost yourself. God forbid!

My brothers and sisters, we walk in confidence knowing all things work together for good and for them that love God. Whatever trials and tribulations that come your way, God will make it work out for your good if your trust lies within Him. Knowing who you are in God puts you in a position to find your destiny's road and this is what God wants for all of His people. Seek Him. Obey Him. Love Him. And in doing all of these you will discover who you are in this world.

Many of us do not know who we are because it means a time of being alone, away from everyone else. Most of us know that the person we are with right now is not the person that we want to grow old with, but we keep them around as a "place holder". Using something generic and without substance to hold the place of an object until the approved substance arrives. Place holders do not allow for growth, and if you are not careful, you start patterning your life after a place holder. This happens to both men and women. We wonder at the ages of 50 and 60 why we still do not know our purpose in life. It is usually because we have never taken time out of our chaotic lives to look into the mirror and discover who we are. If you think that discovering who you are has some type of materialistic value such as the kind of house you want to live in, job you want to have, or car you want to drive, then it will take you even more time to discover who you are.

Fear is the enemy of truth because it freezes us in our current condition and tells us it is perfectly OK to remain in this type of shape. Fear does not want you to know the real you because knowing the real you brings out confidence. A people who are intelligent and confident is the worst fear of any type of establishment because there is nothing you can take from them that will stop them, even after this life their words and deeds will live on. This is the power you have when you know who you are, and you cannot know who you are without the Holy Spirit. Why? Let me explain.

In order for any of us to see ourselves, we need to see a reflection of our current state. Going to a circus and looking at all of the reflections of ourselves in fun house mirrors may be fun but they do very little if we are trying to get an honest reflection of ourselves. We don't use fun house mirrors when we want to make sure we are looking good before we leave the house. Now the mirror in your home or car is limited to only showing your external condition, but if we really want to know who we are, then we need a mirror that can see our internal soul, that mirror my friend is the Holy Spirit. Not only does it show us what our true form is internally, but it also gives us a comparison to true perfection. And it doesn't give us this comparison so that we can take comfort in knowing that we are "a work in progress". It shows us perfection so we may become like it.

I have to believe that without the Holy Spirit acting as the mirror, we would be like vampires in a movie, unable to see our own reflection, unable to change. A person who knows who he is doesn't need to ask someone why he is. When you find yourself asking friends and family to give you constructive criticism, then they only give you what they think your actions should be. For instance, if you were to ask those around me if they felt that I was capable of writing a book, they will probably tell you "No". And if I were to align my actions with what they felt I was capable of doing, then you wouldn't be reading this book right now.

Because it has been revealed to me by the Holy Spirit who I am, I am free to be me and not be shackled by the "who" people think I am. Do you see the power that people could have over you if you don't know who you are?

Many of us are living in houses that are not ours but belong to our friend. We are the ones paying the mortgage, but it was our friends or family's dream that we went out and purchased. Now we are struggling with making the payment because the house was never ours to begin with. I speak of some of us living in houses that don't belong to us but our friends, in addition, some of us are married to spouses that don't belong to us, they belong to our friends.

Do you believe that people who come from a well to do background are free to be who they want to be? Of course not, they have to marry for images so the public is accepting of their spouse. This thought process has been taken on by many of us as well. When you can't be who you are then you have to be someone else until the real approved you arrives on the scene.

Reflection

1. How do you see yourself today? Define the person that you are?

2. If there is anything that you can change about who you are, what would it be? What's holding you back from making that change?

3. Have you lived the life that you want live thus far, or is your life patterned out to somebody else's idea of what it should be? What is your vision for your life?

4. Lists the scripture in this chapter that explains who you are in God.

5. What steps can you take in order to fully accept the above as truth?

Know Who You Are

Reader's Notes

_____

_____

_____

_____

_____

_____

_____

_____

_____

_____

_____

_____

_____

_____

_____

_____

_____

_____

_____

_____

_____

_____

_____

_____

_____

_____

_____

_____

_____

Conception Then Manifestation

If you can understand the process of conception and then manifestation you will discover how God blesses His people. Before the earth was formed, the Lord already had a plan for our lives. God has everything in order and He is in control at all times. Since the beginning of time we have already been blessed because before time existed it has already been seen what we would go through and a perfect design is not created from reaction but by being proactive. In other words, before our time God has already blessed us in His time. If in design He knows all things before they happen, He also already knows what I can bear. The gospels confirm that God would never put anything on us that is more than we can bear. He made a promise in His word that He would never leave us nor forsake us, and He would be there in our times of trouble. He is the beginning of time and He is the end of time.

> *"...I am the Alpha and Omega, the beginning and the end..." (Revelation 21:16 - KJV)*

God is all knowing and before the foundation of the Earth, our Father has already said by His word, that He knows my ups and my downs; He knows whether I am happy or whether I am sad. Because God knows everything about me and I am His child, I need not worry like others worry. My hope is in Him and because of this, He knows when I need Him the most, and He shall be there for me. This is why we should place our trust in Him and not in man. Reader Pay Attention: Because of man's insecurities and inadequacies, it makes for God's opportunities. Do not fret in a time of need because it gives you and others the opportunity to see God work when there is no way it could have been done otherwise.

When we were born into this life we became a part of the corrupt seed which wants to reside inside all of us. This world is corrupt and tainted; it is the world and we live in it. We would have to live in a corrupt world in order for God's power to be seen or manifested in it. Everything in this world will wither away, like the grass in the winter time. The only thing that can bring life to a chaotic world is the Word of God. His words bring life to a dying world. God has to place us in this dark decaying world in order to speak life into it. How is it possible to bring life? You bring life by speaking the Word of God (life) into your situations and circumstances.

People are losing their jobs, homes and financial savings daily. Without seeing what will happen tomorrow we get depressed, but the Word of God says that it has never seen the righteous forsaken or it's seed begging bread. That is the promise God has made to us all. When you speak the word of God it is powerful alone, it only needs one aide... faith.

When you speak the words, you have to place the words over your circumstance in order for change to happen. Not only can it change a circumstance, but it also changes the course of time. When something should die according to man's time, the Word of God brings life to it so it stands erect, and with life and where there is life then miracles are possible. That is the power of the Word, so you have to speak the words if you want things to change.

I often hear people say that God has changed their situation, but we must understand that God gives us the power to change our situation. When we say we are waiting on God we are incorrect. Actually, God is waiting on us. He is waiting on us to use the authority in which He has already given us. God said He made us the head and not the tail and if we are not using that authority, you make yourself the tail of that situation! This is why we get so frustrated with our lives because we fail to understand the power that lies within us.

The Word is so powerful that when it is spoken by any person, it is really like God speaking to Himself. The king's word is sent out to the kingdom by a messenger and though the messenger didn't write the words, when he speaks them, he speaks them with the authority that the king has given him. When God speaks, He speaks from His Word (the Bible). If God says anything to you then He will say it through scripture.

Like a husband and wife joined, God and His word are one. This means that if you are a believer of God, you must also be a believer of His Word. If you are to receive a blessing from God then it will be in accordance with His Word, the Word that He has already spoken. So if God takes it from His Word, which has already been written, that means it was in the Word and ready for you all the time. God did not "just" bless you; He already blessed you because He works in according to His Word. How can we say we are waiting on God to do something when He has already done it?

When the Lord speaks something into the Earth it is not the beginning, but it is the finish of it. If God has spoken, then it is finished. It is impossible to start something that is already completed. Maybe it is a start for us because we are at that time able to see a glimpse of what is happening, but it is the ending touches of God. We are human beings in a natural world and God in His wisdom knows He has to abide by the laws of this land. The scriptures tells us to abide by the laws of the land, therefore God is not going to tell us to do something that He is not able to do.

Time was created as a byproduct for mankind, not for God. This means that God blesses us when it is our time. When God speaks it just doesn't drop from Heaven, but it starts out as a seed. And just like an embryo within its mother has to go through the 9 months of pregnancy and development, at each stage, becoming what we see at delivery. The same is true for our blessings; they too have to go through a similar process. It is not that God does not hear us at times, but we have to just understand that it is not yet the "delivery" time for our blessing. It is important for us all to understand that the Lord, unlike mankind, does not deliver anything prematurely. We as humans try to rush the process, and so we get in a hurry and attempt to do things on our own, and when our blessings are there for us to pick up, we are not there at the delivery time.

What happens to the blessing when we turn away from God? God promised to bless you, you may not have been patient enough for the blessing to fall upon you, but the blessing stays in your generation until someone from your bloodline can sign for it. If you do not see the blessing, rest assured that someone in your generation will receive the blessing. When God delivers a blessing He does not leave a return address so the blessing has to stay on Earth until someone takes ownership of it. If you are waiting on God to act on your behalf, then wait! The seed God has given must manifest itself; it has to come up and it has to be delivered.

Why are God's blessings a process? The Lord must prepare us for His blessings because there is a process in changing a person's state of mind without them going insane. Yes, a sudden change to your mindset could drive you crazy because you would cease to operate in the natural laws of this world. Also, mankind has a tendency to think more of itself than it should when we are blessed. God's wisdom does not want our blessings to overbear us, but He wants us to stay in control of our blessings.

Before you ask God for anything make sure you are patient enough to allow Him to prepare you. God knows us better than we know ourselves. On the same token, if you do not speak things with faith (faith has the power to bring things into existence) then you live beneath the privileges that God has given you. God is waiting for you to change the things that are in your life.

"....You do not have, because you do not ask" (James 4:2 – NKJV)

The seed has already been made into conception by God and now God is waiting for the manifestation to take place by you. All of this is done to let others who are believers know that God is still in control. And it helps nonbelievers know that there is a God, which will help them to believe.

It is important to know the spiritual seed you are carrying because your seed is your destiny. Yes, your seed tells you what direction God is taking you. Like a woman who may be a drinker or smoker finds out that she is pregnant. The woman will most likely stop drinking and smoking in order to protect the child (the seed) within. The same should hold true for us once we find out that God has placed a seed of purpose within us. Evil forces indeed are trying to get you to abort or abandon your seed. He knows that only you, by what you take into yourself or let out of yourself, will cause a miscarriage of this seed. Before there can be any type of purpose there has to be a seed, so recognize your seed. Only when you gain an understanding of who you are and what you are to God does the manifestation start.

You are free. You are powerful. You are more than a conqueror. You have been transformed from being creatures of God to a child of God. Until a person can conceive the greatness which lies within them, they can never start to act upon their greatness.

When we go to work at our places of employment, we know that on payday our checks will be waiting for us. Imagine having to live those two weeks in between pay periods not knowing whether or not you would be paid. For most of us, that would probably be the hardest two weeks of our lives, but this is how most of us live every day when we do not believe the promise that God has already made to us.

Trials and tribulations will come upon us, not necessarily because you have done anything wrong or have sinned, it has already been ordered that they will come upon us. It too has already been ordered that we will conquer our trials in Christ Jesus' name so that we may be a bright beacon to others who are searching for a way out of the darkness.

Someone deceased has you questioning whether or not God exists because He took your loved one after you had prayed so diligently for them to be healed. Have you ever noticed that the good die young and those who are evil seem to live forever? Somewhere along the line we have begun to think that living is the ultimate blessing. And if living here is not the ultimate blessing, but living in Heaven is, it makes all the more sense for the good to die young. I have used this illustration because there are so many of us who can't see beyond the past. Everything around us has stopped working because we have stopped believing the "promise".

"For the promise that he would be the heir of the world was not to Abraham or to his seed through the law, but through the righteousness of faith. For if those who are of the law are heirs, faith is made void and the promise made of no effect, because the law brings about wrath; for where there is no law, there is no transgression.

89

> *Therefore, it is of faith that it might be according to grace, so that the promise might be sure to all seed, not only to those who are of the law, but also to those who are of the faith of Abraham, who is the father of us all (as it is written, 'I have made you a father of many nations') in the presence of Him whom he believed – God, who gives life to the dead and calls those things which do not exist as though they did; who, contrary to hope, in hope believed, so that he became a father of many nations, according to what was spoken, 'so shall your descendants be.' And not being weak in faith, he did not consider his own body, already dead (since he was about a hundred years old), and the deadness of Sarah womb. He did not waver at the promise of God through unbelief, but was strengthened in faith, giving glory to God, and being fully convinced that what He had promised he was able to perform. And therefore 'it was accounted to him for righteousness.' Now it was not written for his sake alone that it was imputed to him, but also for us. It shall be imputed to us who believe in Him who raised up Jesus our Lord from the dead, who was delivered up because of our offenses, and was raised because of our justification."(Romans 4:13-25 – NKJV)*

This scripture tells us that your amount of faith determines your amount of grace and that Abraham is our father because he is the father of faith. God promised Abraham a seed and even when it was seemingly impossible for this type of manifestation to happen in the natural world Abraham still had hope of the conception, which became a manifestation for us all to bear witness to.

The power yielded by faith was not only given to just Abraham, but the scripture tells us it was for his descendants as well. Abraham knew that if God said He would do something, all that he needed to do was to give God the praise and thank Him for having done it. <u>This is a call to understand that the conception comes through hope, but the manifestation comes by faith.</u>

We were told through the scripture that we were all given a measure of faith; all we have to do is tap into it, but how do we?

Christ said we have not because we ask not; therefore anything is possible when we come to God in prayer and it is in His will. If you are reading this literature right now, it is not by chance or circumstance, it is because you have been called by the Lord to do so. Whether you attend church or you do not, the "call" is upon you.

It may be that you have lost hope in living and you cannot see the reason to go on with life, but I ask that you hang on in there. It may be that you have been faithful to a loved one and they have just cheated on you or abused your love and now you see no reason to love again, but I ask that you hang on in there. It may be that people on your job are picking with you and you are fighting off the temptation to return evil for evil, but I ask that you hang on in there. It may have been that you have witnessed people playing the Christian role who were not sincere and it has left a bad taste in your mouth and now you just want to turn away because people have shown you that God must not really exist, but I ask you to hang on in there. Where ever you are, I want you to read the Prayer of Faith below. Read it as if you are reading it to a lover who you are pleading with to stay after you had just been caught being unfaithful to him/her.

Prayer of Faith:

"Dear Lord, I come to you right now unworthy, unholy and unable to see beyond this very second. Father I know by my deeds I have no right to ask you of anything, but I come to you with hope in my heart that I may be changed. Not changed so that I may continue in my own will and with my own understanding, but I ask that you change me Lord so that your will may be done. Father I ask you that the measure of faith that you gave me from the beginning of my conception to be loosened and stirred. I ask that you forgive me of my transgressions as I forgive those who have transgressed against me. Lord I do not know the way to salvation, unless you guide me. My hope, Oh God, is within you; please show your favor upon my life so that I may have salvation. Broken I come to you, but allow me to return anew. Father you said

that you would never leave me nor forsaken me, and though I am not worthy, I know you are worthy to keep your promise to me. These and all other things I ask in your son Jesus' name who died for our sins so that I may have a chance to be free. Amen."

And so it is done. Welcome to the new you!

Reflection

1. We have the power through Christ Jesus to speak into any situation. How does one speak life into a "dead" situation?

2. There is power in God and there is power in His Word. The scriptures included in this chapter speak to us about that very power. Reflect on the scriptures, take a few moments to meditate on them and write out what God has revealed to you about His power.

3. At times it is hard to tap into our faith, but we can increase our faith by trusting in God. Pray the Prayer of Faith and ask God to renew your spirit in Him.

Conception Then Manifestation

Reader's Notes

_____

_____

_____

_____

_____

_____

_____

_____

_____

_____

_____

_____

Bonus Chapter
"Do I Have Faith?"

Throughout the conversation in this book you have noticed that I have used the word "faith" repeatedly. The word "faith" has been defined in the book, and it was told to you that we must have it in order to have this life of peace and joy we are seeking. This chapter is not for everyone because there are those of you who have strong faith, though at times you tend to waiver in difficult times. There are those that tell the world they have faith and won't listen to anyone otherwise, even if they have never applied faith (this chapter is not for you). Lastly, there are those of you who are new in this walk and you have watched people that you thought had faith but they turned their backs on God, and now you're unsure if you really have it.

Do you have faith? You most certainly do, even atheists have a measurement of faith that was given to them. This is what makes everyone accountable on Judgment Day and why there can be no excuses at that time. You have faith, but do you use it and increase it?

There are two things that can be the enemy of faith and cause you to not grow. The first I will speak about is our "Intellect." The more seemingly intelligent we become, the more we rely on our own intelligence or some other person's faith to get us out of tough jams. As long as we can develop a plan or train for mishaps, then we shall forever push faith down. I am not saying that we should not plan, educate or train, but we have failed at our time of need because we have an Ace up our sleeve that guarantees our success; Faith.

Imagine yourself going to college and working hard and then becoming financially successful at the age of 30. You are not rich, but you are comfortable and you budget your money so that when things come up you can always have money to resolve those issues. A person in this type of scenario actually has very little faith, and they have very little faith because they have no need to call on it. The person who is rich has even less faith.

There is a simple phrase I use when I speak in front of congregations, "It takes a situation to cause a revelation". This means that in order for me to have some type of epiphany from God, I am more than likely to have one when a situation has caused me to nearly be broken. It is exactly for this reason the scripture tells us to count it as joy when various trials fall upon us. As much as our intellect can benefit us in our life, it can do just as much harm in our spiritual walk.

The second thing that can handicap our faith is "fear". As mentioned in the previous chapters, Fear is actually the opposite of faith. When you don't have faith you become hardened. If the definition of faith is the substance of things hoped for, the evidence of things not seen, then the definition of fear is the lack of hope. Fear is a mirage without any evidence in a future event. Please understand that when we speak of our natural instincts of "fight or flight", this type of fear was given to us for survival and going forward we shall call this type of fear "awareness".

Awareness is knowing that something exists because you notice it or realize that it is happening because of one of your five senses. Fear is basically non-movement because of something. We have heard the phrase "paralyzing fear"; well it is because fear causes you to stop and not go forward. If there is any movement that will be made, it will be sideways or backwards.

Absolute faith is the non-existence of fear. Fear can even be said to be the desire to preserve yourself or something that you deem important.

Awareness relies on your five natural senses; there is nothing spiritual that takes place with you being aware of things happening around you. Fear in the sense I am speaking of is a spiritual thing, even God said to mankind that He did not give you the spirit of fear.

> *"For I have not given you the spirit of fear, but of love...." (2 Timothy 1:5 – NKJV)*

Fear comes straight from the pits of hell. Fear prevents us from having the ability to walk closer to God by fulfilling our purpose. Fear's only goal is to not allow you to form a closer relationship with God.

In the story of Job, it was fear that Satan used as a tool to try to break Job's faith. Satan's belief was that mankind would turn their backs on God if they could preserve themselves from pain, hurt or death. Absolute faith is the non-existence of fear. How can someone not have any fear?

Have you ever noticed that people seem to die faster when they go to the doctor and they are informed they have cancer? It would appear to me that somehow knowing that they have a disease gives strength to the disease. And it would appear that before they were aware of the disease that most people would say they did not know anything was wrong. Here is an example of ignorance maybe being bliss and not knowing your condition gave you faith that you were "OK", but once you were made aware of the disease then fear seeped in and choked out this faith you once had.

When fear comes in, life goes out. Fear causes us to doubt (some of you may have thought that doubt would be the opposite of fear); not in ourselves, but in God. You already understand what you are capable and incapable of doing on your own, but do you know what your capabilities are when God is your power source? When God is in control of our lives then the rules of physics no longer apply to us. The disciple in the Bible was able to walk across water because he started walking on faith, once he remembered that walking on water should be impossible, it became impossible for him to walk on it.

There has to be a situation for there to be a revelation. Many people, including a lot of teachers, will tell you that in order to have faith it must be a future thing, but I must tell you that faith is a "now" thing! Fear and intellect deal in the future, but not faith. Faith becomes active when there is a situation that you can't handle; it is when you're struggling that you come to understand that there is a power outside of yourself that must come alive.

Imagine, if you can, that you are a professional fighter who has been trained in your profession well. You have an opponent that has won every fight by choking out his opponent. Because you know this, you train especially hard to defend yourself against this type of submission. It is fight night and you are now in the ring and you have defended your opponent so he has not been able to place you in the choke hold, at no time did you use the power of your faith.

Well, at what point would faith be made active? Faith is not in you defending your opponent's attempts to choke you. In order for your faith to be made active then your opponent must have secured the choke hold around your neck and you must have come to the understanding that this is something you cannot get yourself out of, but you continue to hang on and you continue to fight! It is at that point when you get out of the choke hold that the glory must be given to God, for you know within yourself that you could not have gotten out of this deadly move without help. Yes, faith became active when you hoped and you tried to get out of the choke hold though you had never seen anyone else get out of the move.

Instead of a choke hold being applied to you, think about life's trials being the choke hold. The husband that won't evolve and come close to God is a choke hold. The car on the road that slides on ice and you start hoping for survival is a choke hold. The mother that wants a child but her body cannot produce a baby no matter what they have tried in the past is the choke hold. The father who is desperately looking for a job but no one will hire him is a choke hold. The parents that have raised their child the best way they could and their child has forgotten the way they were brought up is the choke hold.

Faith is an inner joy; it is one of the only things that Satan cannot touch. As many of you may understand, Satan's overall goal is to use the things in his control that surround you so that you can lose faith or lessen your faith. He does not have the ability to do this to you. It is something that you must do freely. Is not this what the story of Job in the Bible teaches us? Faith and love are connected. Show me someone who has faith, and I will show you someone who has love. Point out the person that has lost their faith, and I will show you the one who is incapable to love in their current state.

A person can be committed to you without love, they can care for you without love, but they cannot give true encouragement "in spite of" without love. A lot of you are surrounded every day with people who are negative, people who do not move forward and they want to make sure that you do not move forward as well. They may dress themselves in the Christian banner, but they are no more Christians than someone who is an atheist. Negative people lack faith; therefore, negative people do not truly love you. They will poison you with their negativity in the attempt to have you lose hope. Yes, when negativity creeps in, your faith checks out. These are the types of people that you run from.

Though I understand it may not be that easy because many of you by reading this book have come to the understanding that it is your spouse, mother, or children that I spoke of. Do not lose faith, for there is a scripture that I would like to share with you. This scripture will provide protection against all that come up against you. The scripture is Psalms 31. Before you read it ask God to strengthen you, to cleanse you and believe that He will. Do not wrestle in your mind how He will do it, just believe that He will.

There is a time and a place with faith. When you have wondered if you have faith, we are going to discover that there is a time and place that your faith kicks in. Faith is not saying in the future that you will be a millionaire, no, faith starts now when you don't have a dime and you believe you are a millionaire. It is the earlier example of the wrestlers. If I know you are a choke hold specialist and I say I'm going to use faith to beat you. I'm thinking while we are on the mat shifting positions and I am defending myself against your attack that I have called upon faith and that it is already active. This is not correct though, my faith doesn't actually kick in until you have subdued me. When you have been pushed to the point to where you are unable to use anything at your disposal; not your training and certainly not your intellect.

Yes, faith starts when you stop. Once my five senses (the things God gave us to survive in this life) are of no use to me in order to get me out of a predicament, there is faith that acts as the sixth sense. When there is no way you can get yourself out of the enemy's choke hold and you have surrendered over to God - that is when your faith kicks in.

Reader pay attention: Faith is not working when I am using my intellect to figure out how to get out of something and I work out my personal strategic plans. I have to be taken to the point where I understand that I am incapable of going another step without the aid of a higher power. In the Bible there is a story of a lady who had a bleeding disorder for years. She spent years going to doctors to get help, which meant she had money because there were no charity hospitals at the time. After all her money was gone she heard about Jesus and the miracles he was performing. She then said "Oh, if I could just touch the helm of his garment". This woman did touch his garment and the blood instantly began to stop. But you see this woman went from walking with money to crawling with nothing! "Oh, if I could just touch the helm of his garment." The crawling with nothing is when her faith kicked in. God allowed her to spend everything she had in this world so she would be able to get what she needed out of the next world.

We have been taught that faith is a futuristic thing, which means that we believe we are going to be at a certain place in our life. We believe that when we get to a situation that seeks to cripple us, faith won't allow it to happen, but faith is a direction and faith is a time. Most people think "my faith will be there when I get there", but faith starts when you are in trouble because when you are in trouble you allow faith then to direct you and your life. Some of you will say that you have faith that you are going to be married, but in order for faith to become active you have to go through all of the hell of the folks that are not for you and still have hope that your spouse will be there. That is an example of faith for all of you who are ready to give up on relationships.

Ladies, that is why so many of you believe in God for a man, but your lack of understanding of faith causes you to grab on to the first one that comes your way. And then when the relationship doesn't work out you start questioning your faith, but that was not you believing in God, that was you believing in yourself and what you could do.

"Do I have faith?" Well, do you?

Bonus Chapter: Do I Have Faith

Reader's Notes

_____

_____

_____

_____

_____

_____

_____

_____

_____

_____

_____

_____

_____

Coming Soon
Look for these exciting books
by
Darrell Summerville

. . . .

The Power of a Woman's Position

Living Free Within My Relationship

How to Love My Haters

If you would like us to contact you when any of these exciting titles are released, please email me at:
livingfree@authorshippublishing.com

LaVergne, TN USA
05 December 2010
207456LV00002B/11/P

9 780982 151884